When Jesus Comes Back

Carolyn Nystrom

ILLUSTRATED BY EIRA REEVES

Text © 1981 by The Moody Bible
Institute of Chicago
Design © 1993 Tim Douley & Peter
Wyart trading as Three's Company

First published in this edition by
Moody Press in 1994
2nd printing 2002

ISBN: 0–8024–7861–1

Designed and created by
Three's Company, 5 Dryden Street,
London WC2E 9NW
Worldwide co-edition organized and
produced by Angus Hudson Ltd,
Concorde House, Grenville Place,
London NW7 3SA
fax +44 208 959 3678

Printed in Singapore

Moody Press, a ministry of the Moody
Bible Institute, is designed for
education, evangelization, and
edification. If we may assist you in
knowing more about Christ and the
Christian life, please write us without
obligation: Moody Press, c/o MLM,
Chicago, Illinois, 60610.

Long, long ago, before there was a sun or a moon or the stars or the earth, there was God. And God made everything—out of nothing. Because God is God, He can do that.

Then God made people, a man and a woman. And He put those people in a beautiful world full of flowers and birds and oceans and trees and grass and hills and mountains. God visited them there in their beautiful world. In the evening, He walked and talked with them.

God wanted the man and woman to obey Him because they loved Him. So God gave the man and the woman a choice.

The man and woman chose not to obey God. After that, big rocks filled the soft soil. Huge thorns choked the flowers and fruits. The world became a hard place to live.

The world I live in is still a little like the beautiful world God made. Last summer I ran along the ocean beach. I felt soft warm sand squish between my toes. I saw the ocean stretch like a blue blanket all the way to the sky. I saw strong waves splash at rocks as high as buildings and scatter gulls into the white clouds above. And I knew that God had made all this—for me.

4

Then I felt a sharp stab at my foot. I picked up a broken piece of glass and watched blood drip from my heel. And I knew that even the most beautiful scene can become a place of pain.

Luke 2:1–7; John 3:16; Hebrews 2:17–18; Hebrews 4:15; Matthew 5:1–12

Even after God saw the first man and woman disobey Him, God still loved the people He had made. Much, much later, God sent His Son Jesus. Jesus came as a poor person. The night Jesus was born, His parents were staying in a barn. When Jesus grew up He got hot and tired and dirty and hungry and hurt—just like all of us. But Jesus was different in one way. Jesus never did anything wrong.

Jesus helped everyone who knew Him. He made sick people well. He gave food to those who were hungry. He taught them God's laws. Jesus knew that people who obey God's rules are happy with each other. And God is happy with them.

Then Jesus died. People were used to a world that was bad. They were afraid of someone who was all good. So they made fun of Jesus. They pulled sharp thorns from the ground and made a fake crown. They cut down a tree and made its wood into a cross. Then they hung Jesus there until He died.

But Jesus came back to life! He came out of His grave. He walked and talked with His friends. He even cooked breakfast and ate with them. One day as He was teaching, Jesus went straight up into the sky to heaven. While His friends were still watching, an angel spoke. "This same Jesus will come back," the angel said, "just the way you saw Him go."

Ever since that day, people who love Jesus have been waiting for Him.

I am waiting too.

The Bible tells us that the evil that began in the world, when the first man and woman chose not to obey God, will keep on getting worse. Scary times will come. We will see wars and earthquakes and storms. Moms and dads will fight with each other. Children will fight with their parents. The earth will not give enough food for people to eat. Even the moon and stars and sun will not give as much light.

But God will still love us, even then. And
Jesus will come soon.

Wonderful things will happen when Jesus comes back to earth. The Bible says that Jesus will come in the sky, just the way He left.

12

Dead people who loved Jesus will come back to life—just as He did. They will come out of their graves alive and healthy and strong and full of joy. Their bodies will be fresh and new. They will rise up in the air to meet Jesus. Then people who also love Jesus, and are still alive, will go up in the sky with Jesus too.

One day last spring I walked through a cemetery with my mom. We put flowers on my Aunt Sue's grave. A wind chime in the tree sparkled the air with music. A soft breeze carried the smell of fresh earth and new leaves and barnyard animals.

14

Mom and I looked at gravestones. Some people had died more than a hundred years ago. Others had died just this year. Some had lived until they were old. Others had died when they were children. Many gravestones spoke of heaven. The people buried there planned to live again—with Jesus.

Won't it be fun to see all of those people alive again—at the same time?

15

Matthew 24:36–44; Job 19:25–27

When will Jesus come? No one knows. Jesus might wait for thousands of years. Or He might come back today. The Bible says that God wants us to be ready all the time.

I hope I am visiting this cemetery when Jesus comes. It will be exciting to see everyone come back to life. I want to hug my Aunt Sue as we rise up to meet Jesus.

Psalm 139:1–6; Matthew 12:36–37; 1 Corinthians 4:4–5; Romans 2:16

While I wait for Jesus, God sees everything that I do. God saw me help my dad stack wood for winter fires. God knows everything.

God hears everything that I say. God heard me say, "I love you," to baby Seth when I kissed him good night.

God even knows what I think. He knows that I sleep with the blanket over my head because I don't like the dark.

*Psalms 96:10–13; Romans 14:9–12; 2 Corinthians 5:6–10;
Revelation 21:22–27*

Someday I will sit down with Jesus. He will put His arm around me. Jesus will remember everything I have thought and said and done in my whole life. Then Jesus will say, "Jimmy, I love you. I died for you. And you are mine."

Jesus has a book called the book of life. The name of every person who loves Jesus is written in that book. When Jesus opens the book of life He will see my name: Jimmy.

21

We live in a tired world. The soil is wearing out. Too many trees are cut down. Even the sky is smudged with pollution. Plants, trees, animals, and people all die.

22 LITTER

But Jesus is going to make everything new.
Jesus will make a new heaven and a new
earth. And Jesus will live there with His people.
And no one will ever cry again.

2 Peter 3:3–13; Revelation 20:7–10; Revelation 21:6–8, 22–27

Satan tricked the first man and woman. Ever since that time Satan has tried to turn people against God. Satan says, "What God says doesn't matter. You can do whatever you want."

Some people believe this trick. They lie and steal and hate each other. They try to forget about God.

But God will win in the end! God will throw Satan into hell. No one will ever tempt us to do wrong again. And God will be king over everyone and everything, for ever and ever.

Before Jesus died, He talked with His friends. He knew that they would be sad without Him. "Don't be afraid," He said. "I am going to make heaven ready for you. Heaven will have room for everyone. I will come back to take you there."

No one knows exactly what heaven will be like. But if Jesus is making heaven ready for me, I know that I will like it.

Will heaven be full of trees and grass and mountains and waterfalls and oceans and clouds—just like the world God made in the beginning? Will heaven be thousands and millions of stars and planets, each one more fresh and exciting than the last?

I don't know. But if God can make the whole world out of nothing, God can make heaven any way that He wants.

No matter what heaven is, heaven is a forever place. People who love Jesus will live there forever. And forever never ever ends.

At the end of the Bible, Jesus said, "I am coming soon."

I hope so. I want to see Jesus.